Following Jules

Gordon Hartley was born in Rawtenstall, East Lancashire and educated at Giggleswick School and Queens' College, Cambridge. His career began in the textile industry, which took him from Lancashire to Nigeria, Scotland and finally Tanzania. After returning to England he joined what was then the H M Customs and Excise. His last two jobs before retiring were as the Administration Officer for two UK-funded aid projects – in Zambia and Nepal.

He now lives in a village near Lewes, East Sussex and is the author of *The Bandari Contract* and *Mama Beauty*.

Published by G W Hartley

© 2021 United Kingdom

Introduction

My dear wife died in July 2013 and in December I flew to Australia with my brother. We spent Christmas with Brian's youngest son Patrick and his lovely family, at their 'Summer' home along the Great North Road.

Plate 1.

For my Winter holiday the following year I booked a Cunard World Cruise.

I opted for the Southern route and joined Queen Mary 2 on 4 January 2015. Friends and family asked me to let them know how I progressed. I sent a series of emails, which I amalgamated when I got back.

Some pictures and explanatory comments have been added for this record of my voyage.

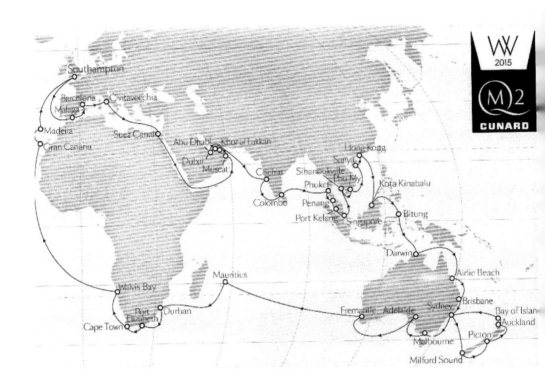

Plate 2.

20 January 2015. Off Port Said, Egypt

So far we have called at **Malaga, Barcelona** and **Civitavecchia**, the port of Rome. I went ashore at Barcelona to do some shopping, but we had often visited Malaga, spent a night in Civitavecchia while driving our car to Malta and have holidayed n Rome. So, I decided my time would be better spent in earning to find my way around this huge vessel.

Plate 3. The Grand Hall.

Since early last night we have been at anchor, about 12 miles outside Port Said (for safety reasons). Yesterday we were given the drill for what would happen in the event of a pirate attack!

The pilots will soon be coming aboard and we are waiting for a build-up of vessels to form a south bound convoy to go through the Suez Canal. However, the Master has just announced that these delays will mean a significant change to our expected arrival time in Aqaba. There are no shore excursions in Egypt (again for safety reasons) but I understand that most of the antiquities of Giza will be visible from the ship.

I have been lucky in the group of six at my dining table --- one other man and four ladies, which is the way I like it! We are all widowed; Ross is a retired horologist from Stirling. Marie-Berthe and Martine are French Canadians who have been friends since childhood, though Martine has lived in Switzerland since her marriage. Marie-Berthe was a nurse who helped her priest brother with his mission hospital in Brazil, so has lots of interesting tales. Myfnanwy Lilyrose is, as you may guess, Welsh. She has been on many cruises and could perhaps be described as 'a free spirit'. Finally, Maria is a former French teacher from Cheltenham, but of Polish parentage. We are all doing the full round trip so I hope we may end up as friends.

Plate 4.

You can imagine my surprise when I bumped into Martyn and Terri Wallwork as I was heading for the Captain's welcome drinks party, for those of us doing the whole trip. They live in

Kingston at the bottom of The Avenue and are getting off at Dubai.

At the moment I have a heavy cold which I think I caught from Lily. (Please don't get the wrong impression, she only came to my stateroom to help me establish this internet connection!)

There will be updates from time to time but I shall now take a walk around the deck.

Sunday, 1st February 2015. In the Indian Ocean, en route to Cochin.

My big disappointment was in not seeing the Suez Canal and the pyramids. We were kept waiting outside Port Said until dusk and then all outside lights were extinguished for safety reasons. Apparently, we entered the canal around 10.30 pm and by dawn we were already cruising the Straits of Suez.

We were offered a compensatory shore visit to **Sharjah**, which didn't interest me. When one goes ashore there is a long queue for passport inspection, which has to be repeated before re-boarding.

I did take a tour of Dubai, which was just as one had been led to expect.. Everything was *'the biggest'*, *'the most expensive'* etc. What I did enjoy was visiting *Ski Dubai* and watching school children pulling each other along on sledges (when the outside temperature was 25 degrees Celsius!) Every Emirati couple is given a free house on marriage and most are rich enough to upgrade to an expensive villa. A return to Dubai on holiday is not for me.

The entertainment has not been very good so far but some new lecturers came aboard at Dubai, including the historian Max Hastings and Sir Jackie Stewart, the racing driver.

I'll be doing a tour of *Cochin* but had hoped we might have visited somewhere more exciting in India. Still, I mustn't complain --- it's warm and sunny on my balcony this morning.

Monday, 9 February 2015

I didn't go ashore in *Abu Dhabi* and those who did said I had not missed much.

Colombo was interesting but not a tourist resort by any means. A lady at my table went on an extended tour to Kandy, which she greatly enjoyed. That is the 'real' **Sri Lanka** --- I once applied for a job tin Kandy and was in the short list, but the mill was never built.

This morning I have been to two interesting talks. The first was about a woman who sailed on the First Fleet to Australia, married, then escaped and got to East Timor before Captain Bligh 'shopped' her and she was returned to England to serve out her sentence. However, she was pardoned due largely to support from James Boswell (Sam Johnson's friend).
Then I went to Sir Max Hastings' last lecture.

Sunday, 15 February 2015. ff Sihanoukville, Cambodia.

We are anchored one and a half miles out because the ship's draft and size make it impossible to moor alongside. Tenders are taking passengers ashore but I'm staying put. Before I left home I saw a TV programme illustrating how Cambodia has constructed a 'sanitised' tour, much as Cuba did when Joan and I called there.

Sihanoukville is a recent small holiday development and there are no tours offered to Phnom Penh, which is the place I wanted to see. However, the two French-Canadian ladies at my table have gone on a two-day overland tour to Ankhor Wat and will re-board in Vietnam. I had thought of doing this but considered it may be a bit much for an 83-year-old, (plus the extra cost would finance a nice holiday in UK!)

Joan and I visited **Penang** in 1972 when we were on a cargo ship. On that trip we went around in a rickshaw! I knew things would have changed a lot and I wouldn't know my way round, so I took one of the tours. Penang is now is a prosperous city, with high-rise developments. This is, of course, a good thing for Malaysia, but the modern tourist can no longer discover the character and charms of what was an old colonial outpost.

I knew **Singapore** would also be much changed since our last visit. Every year they import shiploads of rock and ballast from Malaysia and Indonesia and build out into the sea to make the island larger. In 1972 we walked from Raffles Hotel back to our ship. Now it would be a fifteen-minute taxi ride.

My tour began with a cruise up the river; then we visited a 'multi-faith' temple.   It is shared by Taoists, Buddhists and Confuscionists, each with their own section (if only there could be such a place in Northern Ireland.) Then we went up in their equivalent of the 'London Eye', the first time I have had such an experience. I commented to our guide how proud Lee Kwan Yew would have been of what Singapore has achieved. She replied, 'Oh yes, he *is*." (He is still alive and in his nineties.)

Singapore was the end of a 'leg' of the voyage. There was a major exodus of European and Indian guests and they were replaced mainly by Chinese, who I suspect will get off in Hong Kong, probably to be replaced by Aussies and Kiwis.

We have new lecturers. Max Hastings and Jackie Stewart have left us, replaced by a rocket scientist, a child psychologist, the former chairman of Christies America, plus the TV journalist Dermot Murnaghan. Yesterday I went to a nice classical concert by a Polish clarinet and piano duo.

I am having a great time but sorely missing the lady who should be with me.

Tuesday, 24 February 2015. En route to Borneo.

This was my fourth visit to **Hong Kong** and this was to be only a short. So instead of taking a tour, headed for the shops. I did not buy a digital camera, finding the prices higher than the UK guidelines given by Chris and Alex, but did a little clothes shopping at an emporium called Marks and Spencer.

It was sad to see the lights of the former protectorate disappearing into the distance (in pouring rain).

We lost most of the Chinese at HK but 600 new ones came aboard, plus 1000 Australians. Only just over 200 of us are doing the full voyage and we are to be treated to a special dinner when we reach New Zealand. This is a 'black tie' event at the Auckland Domain and War Memorial Museum and I'm told to expect some excellent food and fine wines.

When we reach Aucklland I am due to be met by Kathy Scarborough, a friend we made when we sailed back from Melbourne in 1997 on the *Oriana*. She is kindly going to give me a personal tour of the city.

In Brisbane I hope to see Gillian Taylor, the daughter of my late cousin Geoffrey. In Melbourne, of course, I shall see Gill and Pat and the girls, plus (hopefully) Brian.

I've just booked a tour of Kota Kinabalu for when we reach Borneo and don't quite know what to expect --- hope I don't encounter any head hunters!

Yesterday I ventured for the first time to one of the 'solo' passengers' get-togethers, lured by the prospect of free champagne. I hoped for a little friendly conversation. Instead I found what can only be described as a 'dating agency'. A large circle of chairs was laid out and a microphone was being passed round where one was expected to give a personal resume and list one's hobbies. As you will no doubt guess, I quickly made my excuses and left!

Its a lovely day today, so I'm now going onto my balcony for a bit of gentle sun bathing.

Monday, 2 March 2015. At sea, en route to Darwin.

Kota Kinabalu in Borneo was a pleasant surprise, a prosperous garden city with lovely floral borders and 'topiarised' trees. It used to be called Jesselton and is the principal town of Sabah province. It has many lovely modern buildings --- sadly, this is due to much of the town being destroyed by heavy bombing by Allied planes during occupation by the Japanese.

Our next port of call, **Bitung** in Indonesia was not so inviting. We were the largest ship ever to dock there and the principal attraction was the amazing welcome one received from the local people, to whom our visit was a major landmark for their town.

I was, surprisingly, invited to join the Captain's table for last night's dinner, Since this was preceded by a cocktail party for those of us doing the whole journey, I was careful to have only one glass of champagne there! I was seated between Carol, the Medical Officer, and Lady Rosalind Dulverton (*call me 'Yottie'*). After the main course the Captain, Christopher Wells, changed places with Carol, so I had a good chat with him. He is leaving us at Darwin and the next Captain will take us home to Southampton. (I am on the right of the picture.)

QUEEN MARY 2
Captain's Table
1 March 2015

Plate 5.

We have a new set of speakers now, including the TV comedy writers Dick Clement and Ian la Frenais who wrote *The Likely Lads, Auf Weidersehen Pet, Lovejoy* etc.

I am particularly enjoying the talks of the royal historian, Prof. Charles Carlton, who yesterday gave us a rundown of royal mistresses, including Nell Gwynne and bringing us up-to-date to include a lady whose name it would not be proper for me to mention! Today I am going to hear Ronald Marks, a former CIA spy.

After breakfast I walked a mile round the deck so am now heading for a nice cooling lemonade.

14 March 2015. In the Tasman Sea, en route to New Zealand.

After a spate of 'foreign' ports it was something of a relief to arrive at **Darwin** and hear a recognisable version of English. The 'Top End', as Australians call the Northern Territory, has a fragile climate and has suffered regular cyclones and many earthquakes. We moored near enough for a pleasant stroll into the city-- more like a 'town' in its size; the whole area having a population of only around 200,000. However, the heat and humidity discouraged me from having a long stay. A pleasant place though. (A Brisbane resident I was talking to said they came up here to escape their 'winter'.)

At Darwin, Captain Wells was replaced by Captain Oprey and we took a specialist pilot on board for the four-day passage through the **Great Barrier Reef**.

Then we moored off Airlie Beach on **Whitsunday Island**, so-named by Captain Cook on that day in 1770 when he was exploring the Queensland Coast, though apparently he never landed there. Our visit was also on a Sunday and it was nice to see that many local volunteers in the lovely settlement had turned out to help us with advice and directions. (I even found a Woolworths for those little essentials not available on board.) Our visit meant that, temporally, we more than doubled the population of Airlie Beach. I arrived on the ship's (lifeboat) tender, but travelled back by catamaran --- another first for Gordon!

On 10th March we arrived at ***Brisbane*** for an all-too-short visit of eight hours. I did not actually see the city because I spent my time with Gillian and John Taylor. She is the daughter of my late Cousin Geoffrey.

Plate 6.

Plate 7. Gillian and John's house

They kindly picked me up from the ship and took me to their charming home-town of Redcliffe, noted as the place where the brothers Gibb, of the *Bee-Gees*, grew up and started the career which made them international pop stars. They took me to their lovely (*old Australian*) home. I felt I had been transported England when we travelled through 'Margate' and 'Scarborough', to have lunch at a seaside restaurant. All too soon it was time for them to return me to the ship. By then I was almost hoarse with talking too much; about family and Lancastrian memories --- a grand day out as we say 'oop North.'

After another sea-day we arrived at *Sydney.* This is the end of a 'leg' of the voyage. There was a mass exodus of passengers and a compensating influx for the next leg, which takes us to NZ and back to Sydney. The big bonus was that we were moored within 200 yards of the Opera House and the Harbour Bridge.

Plate 8.

Plate 9.

I booked myself on the '*Leisurely*' tour of the city so that I could see which parts I will revisit on our return to Sydney. We drove through most of the districts which had previously been just names to me and we spent about forty minutes at Bondi Beach This is a beautiful city which I'm greatly looking forward to seeing again.

The Tasman Sea is now very rough and we are warned of typhoons, which may require revision of our itinerary in New Zealand. Also internet connection is very slow so it may be a day or so before this gets through. Oh for my 'good old days' in Africa and a messenger with a cleft stick!

18 March 2015. At sea, en route to Auckland

Since leaving Sydney the ship has been playing cat and mouse with Cyclone Sam, which has wrought such destruction in Vanuatu. Our first destination was to be the New Zealand fjord region, a World Heritage site. I wondered whether we would be able to get there.

Despite heavy seas, the pilot proved able to guide us safely through the entrance to Milford Sound and the weather improved for our arrival.. We experienced this awesome scenery in bright sunshine. The massive mountains surrounding the Sound rise to over 13,000 feet but, being well wooded, give a less austere impression than those I have seen in the Norwegian fjords. Milford Sound is large and the depth of the water is 300 metres, so this huge vessel had no difficulty in turning full circle to continue our journey. However, the weather came down as we left and the rest of our tour of the fjords was observed through my stateroom window!

Our next target was Akaroa, where we were to have lain at anchor and visited by tender, but the sea conditions were deemed too rough, so an alternative destination was sought (*any port in a storm*). Finally the small town of **Picton** was decided upon (population 3,000), allowing me another cliche . . . *it's an ill wind that blows nobody any good!*

Plate 10. Leaving Picton

We were in Picton yesterday and it was good to get one's feet on New Zealand soil. We were able to draw alongside a large berth, usually devoted to the collection of timber, huge piles of which were stacked along the jetty. It was a pretty place, but a quick wander up and down the main street was all I required. However, a sign outside a pub amused me.
Day centre for husbands, please collect by 1 a.m.

By now we should have arrived in Wellington, where I had booked a tour, but the Captain announced while I was having breakfast that last night's Force Ten gales had made him and the Wellington pilots agree that we must miss our visit to the capital city. We are now proceeding direct to Auckland and he will be informing us of a projected arrival time.

Plate 11. The breakfast room.

Queen Mary 2 was designed as an ocean liner rather than a normal cruise ship, so it was built to cope with Transatlantic gales. What would have been a 'major buffeting' last night in many cruise liners, was reduced to a 'noticeable sway'.

Nevertheless, there was quite a reduction in the number of people coming for breakfast!

Of course, I am disappointed by these alterations to the itinerary but that is being selfish. Vanuatu, and probably other Pacific islands, stand as a rebuke to me.

Sunday, 22 March 2015. At anchor in the Bay of Islands, New Zealand

Having had our planned visits to Akaroa and Wellington cancelled, it was a relief that the cyclone appeared to have blown itself out in time for us to enter the majestic *Auckland* harbour ,soon after 3 pm on last Thursday.

Unfortunately, the *Queen Victoria* had beaten us to it and was safely ensconced in the main cruise berth almost in the city centre, leaving us to moor alongside the quay usually assigned to container vessels.

Plate 12. Berthed in Auckland

However, our ship ran a 'shuttle' bus service into town, so the next morning I was able to meet my friend Kathy Scarborough. (We met Kathy and Tony when we travelled back on the *Oriana* from Melbourne in 1997 and have kept in touch. They came to see us in Kingston when they were in UK for a short spell.)

Plate 13. Kathie and Gordon on Mount Eden

She showed me around the city and its environs far more thoroughly than any of the 'official' tours would have done. Her son Matthew left work for a few minutes to meet me, before we set off on our tour. He is now 23 and, having graduated with a first-class degree, has secured a post with Goldman Sachs. Kathy's twin girls, Hayley and Nicola, have just started university so I didn't meet them again.

Kathy took up her 'tourist guide' duties again the next day, for me and three lady friends. She made my visit to Auckland a memorable occasion and I am most grateful.

A Maori fun night.

On the evening of the 20th there was a special celebratory dinner for those of us who are completing the full World Tour. Having dressed up in our best bib and tucker we were picked up by coaches and taken to the "Auckland Domain and War Memorial Museum". Dinner was preceded by cocktails in the museum entrance hall. Then a 'haka' was performed and the Captain was challenged by a Maori Chief. The Maori group then performed songs and dances until it was time for us to go up to the top floor, where tables for eight were set out for the sumptuous meal. This was followed by dancing, but by11.45 pm your correspondent was safely back at the ship and tucked up in bed!

Today we arrived in the beautiful **Bay of Islands** and I have just returned from a trip, by tender, to the mainland town of Pahia, where a bus took me to the small town centre. The driver assured us we would not get lost provided we kept to the main street, since this was the only street!

I then visited the Waitangi Treaty grounds. It was here that the treaty was signed in 1841 between the Maori chiefs and the British Crown, establishing the place they called 'New Zealand.' It is still a contentious issue, though one observes that the Maori appear to be reasonably integrated within the NZ community.

Across the bay is the town of Russell, which became the first capital of NZ, before Auckland and now Wellington. I shall be sorry to leave this lovely country but am very happy to have had this opportunity to see it.

This evening we will set off back to Sydney, with two days at sea, so I will conclude this chapter of the 'cruise report'. For those of you who can stand to read more, a further email will begin what is essentially 'homeward bound'.

2 April 2015. Maundy Thursday (my 57th wedding anniversary)

At sea, en route to Mauritius

Approaching **Sydney** for a second time was like coming back to meet a new friend and I enjoyed just wandering around the welcoming city. I spent most of my time in the Rocks area, which is where the survivors of the 'First Fleet' were set to work, preparing material for building the original settlement. The new intake of passengers amounts to around 1600 people and we set off along the southern coast of Australia with a fresh set of Aussies, who had flown to Sydney to take the opportunity to sail back to their home towns in luxury.

Melbourne had been my number one target, because I would be seeing my nephew Patrick and family in their new home. Sadly, this was to be a short stop --- dock at 8 am, sail at 4.30 pm. I had to wait an hour for a taxi. The cricket World Cup final was to take place that weekend so drivers were concentrating on the airport run. There was also a gridlock in the city because of the funeral of a former PM, Malcolm Fraser. As a result it was two hours before I reached the Malvern district, where my family live. Pat came out at once to open the taxi door for me. Brian and I had seen their new house partially completed when we left in February last year. The finished product is all one hoped it would be.

Plate 14. Olivia in the kitchen area, with Lily on the sofa.

This was the first day of the holidays for Charlotte and Olivia and it was great to see them both again (The latter still recovering from her previous night's 'sleepover', which I guess did not involve much sleep!)

Plate 15.

There was proof that dogs have long memories when Lily jumped up to sit beside me as soon as I sat down.

Plate 16.

This was a working day for both Gill and Patrick, but Gill came home to see me. Pat and the girls delivered me back to the ship in time for a late lunch, as he had an appointment that afternoon to see his chief, who was flying in from Canberra.

This was a brief but delightful family day.

Adelaide had a much more 'homely' feel than did Sydney and Melbourne. My tour took me through suburbs with bungalows and small shopping arcades rather than the 'posh' areas I saw in the larger cities. We spent half an hour at Glenelg, a seaside resort which reminded me of 1950s England. For a pedant like me, its other attraction was being the first palindrome I can remember visiting!

Adelaide city centre has a splendid cultural centre. The University boasts three Nobel Prize winners. These include Howard Florey, who won his for the development of penicillin, along with Alexander Fleming and Ernst Chain. (Chain was Brian's predecessor as Professor of Biochemistry at Imperial College.)

We were due to leave Adelaide at 6 pm last Sunday but the usual inspection in port showed a fault in the 'screw'. Divers spent the night correcting the fault, which meant we did not sail until 10.30 the next morning. The Captain assured us that he would make up lost time during our two days at sea and that we would arrive at Fremantle on schedule. The Great Australian Bight is home to 'the Roaring Forties' and has a reputation akin to the Bay of Biscay, so the extra speed led to a quite noticeable sway. It was not unpleasant to be *rocked in the cradle of the deep* after a Captain's cocktail party. However, there was once again not the usual crowd for breakfast in the buffet!

There have been few signs of a build-up to Easter; certainly I have seen no evidence of anyone taking a Lenten fast! There is a Roman Catholic priest who spends his whole life on Cunard ships --- a tough life, but somebody has to do it! (Probably his main role is to minister to the 500 strong crew, the majority of whom seem to be from the Philippines.) There are also announcements in the *Daily Programme* of a Seder dinner, for the Jewish community tomorrow to celebrate Passover.

Today we called at **Fremantle,** the port for Perth. Joan and I were here years eighteen ago and, like most visitors, went straight off to Perth.

Plate 17.

So I've spent my time exploring Fremantle itself. It was established before the city, in the (comparatively) far off 1820's, and I accessed it by 'courtesy tram'.

Plate 18.

"OLD" FREMANTLE.

This has been a lovely way to say goodbye to Australasia . . . or should that be *au revoir*?

Saturday, 18 April 2015 In Cape Town

After Fremantle there were six sea days and we reached *Mauritius* on 9th April.

Plate 19. Mauritius harbour.

I did not go ashore there. Joan and I had already visited Mauritius twice and the advertised tours covered what I'd already seen. Port Louis, the capital, is a noisy mess of a place. Added to which we were warned that the local taxi drivers' union had put a 'veto' on a shuttle bus service. The beach resorts north of Port Louis are what draw most visitors to the island and the town of Curepipe in the hills is of some interest. As Dr Johnson said of the Devil's Causeway, it is "*Worth seeing but not worth going to see*". I was happy to have the ship almost to myself for a day.

The classical music duo who joined us in Mauritius are two talented young women called Rosie Reed (flute) and Sarah Kershaw (piano). There could not be a more Lancastrian name than 'Sarah Kershaw' and when we met in one of the tea rooms she told me that she came from a village called Wycoller near Colne . . . did I know it? I was able to tell her that one of our ancestors, Piers Hartley, lived at Wycoller Hall in (I think) the 16th century. Furthermore, I am related to Wallace Hartley, also of Colne, who was the band-master on the *Titanic*.

Then it was another three days at sea until I was again in the continent which we had come to know so well.

Back in Africa.

13th April 2015. Durban.

Having called at Durban with Joan twice on our way home by sea, and having spent a week in the area, to see the David Whitehead and Sons cotton mill in nearby Tongaat, I chose not book a tour.

Plate 20. Gordon and Joan at the David Whitehead Tongaat mill

Plate 21. Joan with Jack Edwards

Instead I went to a new tourist 'village' shopping development called *uShaka* and spent an hour or so at the aquarium, quite the best I have ever visited. I did not exactly dip my toes into the Indian Ocean but it was great to be back on those lovely beaches, especially now that one does not have to decide whether one is sitting at a 'black' or a 'white' bench!

After leaving Durban we encountered heavy weather again, arriving in **Port Elizabeth** on a cold, wet day. We came here in the 1970s on our way down from Tanzania to join the Union Castle ship *Oranje* to take us home on leave. I could not remember the place and realised why --- it is an unmemorable city. Port Elizabeth is now the home of the SA motor industry. Hundreds of VW Polos were parked on the dockside, awaiting shipment to Europe.

Then we had another day and a half at sea, experiencing the roughest weather yet. The stabilisers were out all the time and the Captain said he was constantly changing course to avoid the worst of the storms. We were due in *Cape Town* at 6 am yesterday but the wind speeds were 30 to 40 knots as we approached Table Bay. We waited until the wind dropped to 20 knots before the pilot would come aboard. It was therefore 9.30 am before we finally docked. The weather quickly improved.

We had a lovely sunny day yesterday and I took a tour to the wine-growing town of Stellenbosch. It is also a universiy town. little changed since I last saw it, 40 years ago!

This morning I took the shuttle bus to the Victoria and Alfred waterside complex with a nice Scottish lady I met at breakfast yesterday.

Plate 22.

I have arranged for her to join our table tonight, replacing a woman who joined us at Adelaide.   She has had an interesting life. Having been trained as a fashion model, she married a tea planter who took her out to live in Assam. But they divorced and later she reurned to modelling. This led on to becoming the perfume and cosmetics buyer for House of Fraser's Scottish and Irish branches.

She had boarded in New Zealand where she had been visiting her daughter, whose husband owns a sheep farm.

Only a fortnight remains now and there will be lots of sea days. The remaining calls will be at Walvis Bay in Namibia, Gran Canaria and Madeira, before we reach Southampton on 3rd May.

Thursday, 30 April 2015. At sea, homeward bound

We reached *Namibia* on 20th April. This country was formerly a protectorate of South Africa and before that was German West Africa. As I recall from my days in Tanzania the Kaiser intended to create a link with Tanganyika (German East Africa). This was never achieved and there were fierce disputes over the 'Caprivi Strip'. Maureen and I took a tour from Walvis Bay to Swakopmund, still very much a German town, as evidenced by the names on the shops and some of the street names, though most of the latter had been renamed for heroes of the Independence struggle. The majority of the country comprises the Namib Desert and we travelled through parched territory, stopping at *Dune 7* a high permanent sand dune. Young men were climbing and sliding down on metal trays. You will see them outlined on the skyline in this picture.

Plate 22.

Despite its isolation Swakopmund turned out to be something of a metropolis, yet retained characteristics of its colonial past. Maureen and I had lunch in the dining room of the best hotel, overlooking a courtyard which took my mind back to Anita Brookner's *Hotel du Lac*.

Then we had seven days at sea. Although I had a good book to read (Fay Weldon's *Kehua!*) one must depend on the ship's entertainment during these long sea days, and the evening shows are not to my taste. However, there is a choice of films either in the cinema or on one's stateroom TV. We have a new classical music duo and new speakers on board for the remainder of the voyage.

The keynote speakers now are Michael (now Lord) Howard and his wife Sandra, formerly Sandra Paul the 1960s fashion model and now a popular novelist. They are both interesting and do not keep aloof from the 'plebs', often being seen in the buffet fighting for their breakfast along with us mere mortals.

At last we reached *Gran Canaria* and docked in Las Palmas, a place Joan and I used to visit when travelling on the Elder Dempster line between Liverpool and Lagos.

Plate 23.

We docked at 9 am and were to be back on board by 4.30 pm, so Maureen and I did not book a tour. The ship moored close enough for us to meander through the town, none of which seemed familiar to me (though how could it be after over 50 years?) Maureen persuaded me to buy a 'man-bag'!

Funchal must rank as one of the loveliest island capitals in the world.

Plate 24.

We arrived in Madeira this morning and sailed at 5 pm. It has been a lovely sunny day, full of memories for me. Joan and I first visited by sea in 1963, on our way back on holiday from Nigeria. We returned in 2002, the last land-based holiday we had before her dementia set in. My three remaining table-mates decided to go up to see Reid's Hotel but I looked for a little restaurant which we always used to visit. I was delighted to find it unchanged. I got there too early to eat, so I just had a beer and returned to the ship for lunch.

Now I will soon be in home waters, having two days at sea and arriving in Southampton on Sunday morning.

I will have travelled almost 37,000 nautical miles and visited fourteen countries. I have met family and old friends and I have made new friends. Could this be my swan song? We shall see!

Home sweet home.

Plate 25

Thanks for keeping up with my adventures,

Gordon

Kingston-near-Lewes BN7 3LL, East Sussex.

Printed in Great Britain
by Amazon